SOCCER TACTICS

AN ANALYSIS OF ATTACK AND DEFENSE

Library of Congress Cataloging - in - Publication Data

by Lucchesi, Massimo
SOCCER TACTICS • An Analysis of Attack and Defense

ISBN No. 1-890946-44-3
Library of Congress Catalog Number 00-104668
Copyright © June 2000

Originally printed in Italy - 1999 by Edizioni Nuova Prhomos Via O. Bettacchini. Translated by Sestiltio Polimanti

Art Direction/Book Layout
Kimberly N. Bender

Editing and Proofing
Bryan R. Beaver

Printed by
DATA REPRODUCTIONS

Cover Photograph
EMPICS

REEDSWAIN INC
612 Pughtown Road • Spring City • Pennsylvania 19475
1-800-331-5191• www.reedswain.com

To my wife Stefania and to my children

This book would never have been published without the support of my parents, Liliana and Giuliano.

I would also like to give special recognition to the following clubs: Nuove Leve Massarosa, U.S. Bozzano and C.G.C. Viareggio. Thanks to them I have been able to coach and to gain important professional experience. Special thanks also to Mr. Michelotti and Mr. Del Bucchia (Nuove Leve), Mr. Luporini and Mr. Evangelisti (Bozzano), Mr. D'Angelo and Mr. Barsanti (C.G.C. Viareggio). They have always been helpful to me and have shown their faith in me. I have shared with them joys and disappointments.

Finally, many thanks to all the players I have coached. Their involvement, patience and sacrifices have been instrumental in my improvement as a coach.

Massimo Lucchesi

SOCCER TACTICS

AN ANALYSIS OF ATTACK AND DEFENSE

Published by
REEDSWAIN INC.

Legend ii

Introduction: Tactical Analysis 1

Chapter One: The Offensive Phase 2
  1.1 When the Player Does Not Have the Ball 4
  Analysis of the Player's Functions When Not in Possession 5
  How to Receive the Ball 12
  Movements of the Player Without the Ball 22
  Two Teammates' Supporting Movements 24
  Possible Combinations of a Forward and a Midfielder 27
  1.2 When the Player Has the Ball 30
  Options of the Player Who Has the Ball 31
  Dribbling the Ball: Specific Analysis 35
  1.3 Offensive Subphases 36
  Definition and Objectives of the Offensive Subphases 37
  After Gaining Possession of the Ball 38
  Building up play 39
  Final Touches 50
  Shooting 62

Chapter Two: The Defensive Phase .66
  Definition and Objectives of the Defensive Subphases 68
  Role of the Player Involved in the Defensive Phase 69
  2.1 The Player Facing An Opponent Who Has the Ball . . .70
  How to Tackle the Opponent 71
  Possible Options When Tackling the Opponent Who Has the
  Ball 73
  When to Give Space 74
  **2.2 The Defensive Player Not Facing the Opponent with
  the Ball** 76
  The Passive Player 78
  The Active Player 82
  The Player Aiming at Stealing the Ball 86
  The Player Doing Tactical Work 88
  2.3 Organizing the Defensive Phase 90
  How to Organize the Defensive Phase 91
  Off-side Tactics 96
  Countering the Offense's Final Touches 97

Conclusion 101

Legend

 Player

 Player with the ball

 Orientation of the team to be coached

 Pass

 Movement of the player receiving the ball

1, 2.... Phases of the movement of the ball

 Movement with the ball

 Flag or cone (point of reference)

1   1 Goalkeeper

2   2 Right side back

3   3 Left side back

4   4 Left center midfielder

5   5 Central back

6   6 Right center back

7   7 Right wing

8   8 Left side midfielder

9   Center forward

10   Right side midfielder

11   Left wing

All the following exercises, tactical examples, situations and schemes can of course be applied and used in a mirror-like way in the part of the field opposite to the one shown in the diagrams.

INTRODUCTION
TACTICAL ANALYSIS

Scheme of the phases in soccer

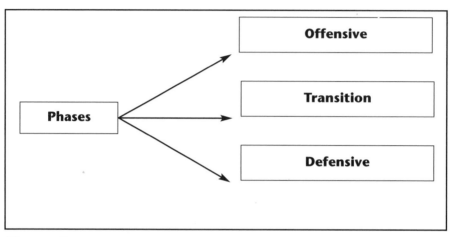

Diagram 1

Definition of the phases:
- The term "offensive phase" refers to when the team has the ball.
- The term "defensive phase" refers to when the team does not have the ball.
- The term "transition phase" refers to the short period of time immediately following the moment when the ball is won or lost, therefore to the change from one phase of play to the other.

The objectives of the various phases:
- In the offensive phase the objective is to score.
- In the defensive phase the objective is to win the ball.
- In the transition phase the objective is to adapt quickly to the new situation.

CHAPTER ONE
THE OFFENSIVE PHASE

The objective of the offensive phase is to score.

The necessary phases which lead to scoring are:
1. Refraining from losing the ball (avoid risky moves in the defensive area).
2. Taking the ball forward towards the opponents' goal.
3. Getting the ball to a teammate who is free from his opponent's marking, placing him in a position to shoot.
4. Shooting effectively.

Statistical analysis has determined that 65% of goals are scored in dynamic play, while 35% are scored in, or following, dead ball situations. Analysis of goals which result from dynamic play shows that the fewer the number of passes, and the shorter the duration of the attack, the more likely the chances of scoring.

Therefore, the offensive team should optimize its time on offense, taking advantage of its players' movements, passing, receiving and shooting skills, to take actions in a quick and decisive way.

On offense, the player with the ball can either kick it (pass it or shoot) or dribble it (also dribbling past an opponent), while his teammates are moving without the ball. The role of the players without the ball are as follows.

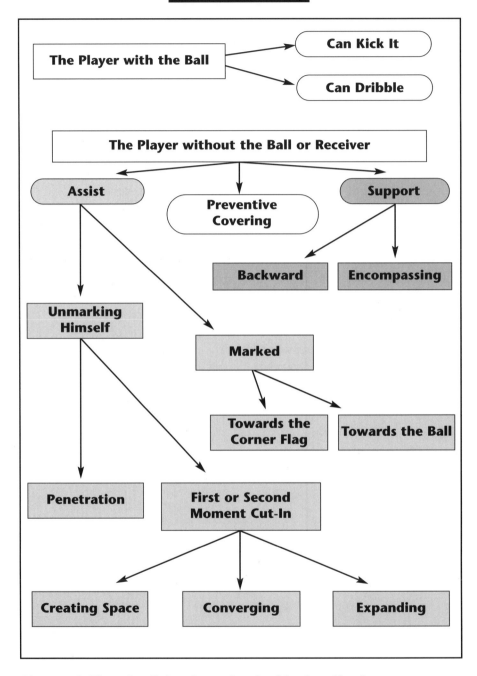

Diagram 2: The role of the players involved in the offensive phase.

1.1 WHEN THE PLAYER DOES NOT HAVE THE BALL

- Analysis of the player's functions when the player does not have the ball.
- How to receive the ball.
- Movements of the player without the ball.
- Supporting movements by two teammates.

In modern soccer, the ability of the offensive player to play without the ball has become more and more important. Considering that in a 90-minute match, the real playing time is hardly ever more than 60 minutes and that there are 20 players (goalkeepers not included) on the field, each player's average time of possession of the ball is 3 minutes. This is why we should be aware of how important it is to make the right tactical choices for the 57 minutes when the player moves without the ball.

Analysis of the player's functions
when not in possession

- **Preventive Covering.**

The offensive players who remain positioned between the opponent's offensive section and the offense's own goal, so as to become an obstacle to the opponents' action if they gain possession of the ball and start an attack, are said to be in preventive covering. All the players on offense who remain positioned behind the line of the ball, are considered to be in "preventive covering".

In diagram 3, the team in black has 4 players, plus the goakeeper, positioned in preventive covering.

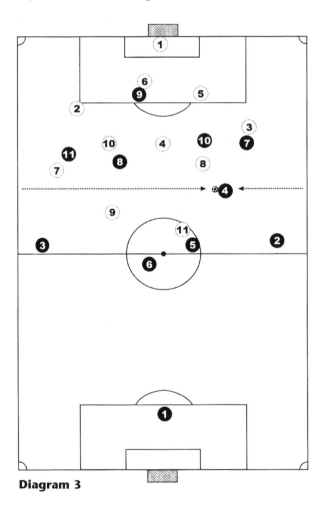

Diagram 3

• Support.

An offensive player who makes himself available for a back pass or a horizontal pass is referred to as a "supporting player".

The supporting player can be termed as "back support" when he is behind the teammate with the ball.

When the supporting player is along the same line as the teammate who has the ball, his support is referred to as "encompassing" because he can receive the ball either some yards forward or some yards back, depending on the game situation.

This kind of positioning is important to enable the teammate with the ball to pass it forward or back, and thus avoid having to pass it horizontally, which can be risky if the opponents intercept it.

In diagram 4, in a 4-player defense, the right central back acts as a back support to the teammate with the ball.

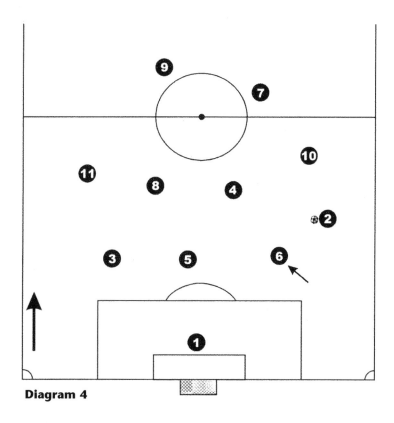

Diagram 4

In diagram 5, in a team arranged according to the 4-4-2, the central midfielder 8 acts as an encompassing support as he can receive the ball either backward or forward.

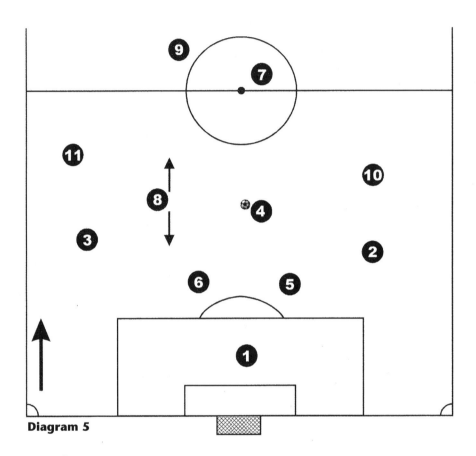

Diagram 5

- **Assist.**

An offensive player who helps to take the ball towards the opposing goal by making himself available for a pass forward, is referred to as an "assisting player".

He can receive the ball in two ways: either with the opponent at his back or by unmarking himself.

He has the opponent at his back when he comes towards the ball or when he cuts towards the corner flag. He tries to receive the ball unmarked when he cuts towards the opposing goal or when he penetrates to receive the pass from his teammate.

Diagram 6 shows how an assisting player, even if marked, comes towards the ball and receives it, thus helping to make it go forward.

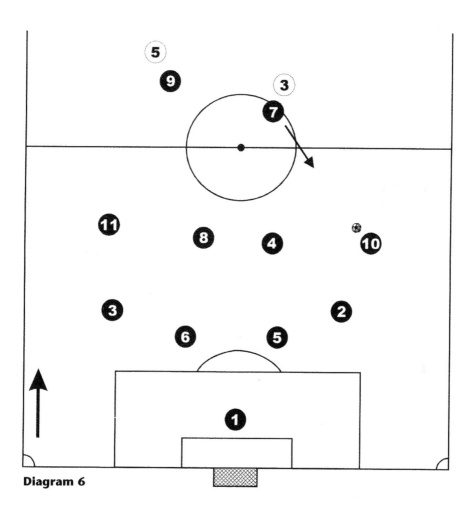

Diagram 6

In diagram 7 the assisting player, even if marked, helps to take the ball forward by cutting towards the sideline.

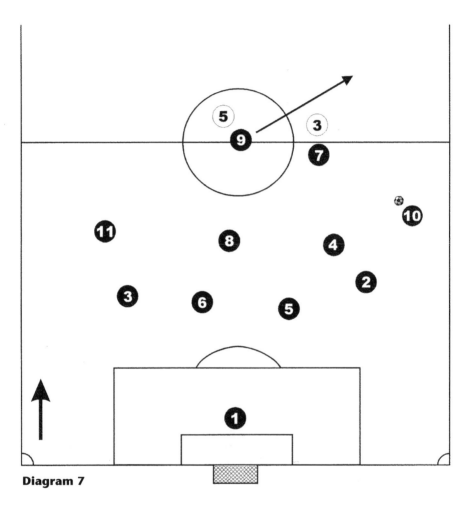

Diagram 7

In diagrams 6 and 7 we have shown assisting movements by the two forwards, but of course any teammate can act as an assisting player.

Diagram 8 shows an example of assisting movements with both a first and a second movement cut-in. While the forward who is closer to the ball goes towards it and creates space, the other forward carries out a converging cut-in, trying to shake off his marker in order to receive a penetrating pass, placing himself in a position for a shot on goal.

At the same time, the left side midfielder carries out a second movement - a vertical cut-in - exploiting the space created by the movement of the forward (the team is arranged according to the 4-4-2).

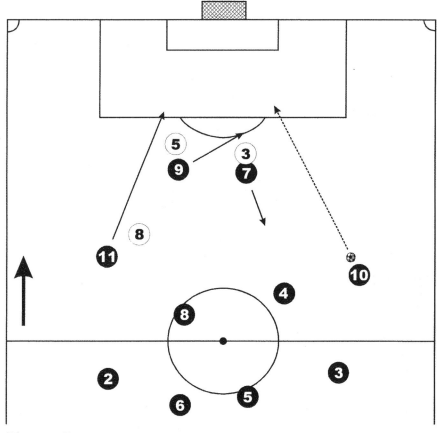

Diagram 8

Diagram 9 shows an assisting penetration by the central midfielder who receives the pass from the forward (team arranged according to the 4-4-2).

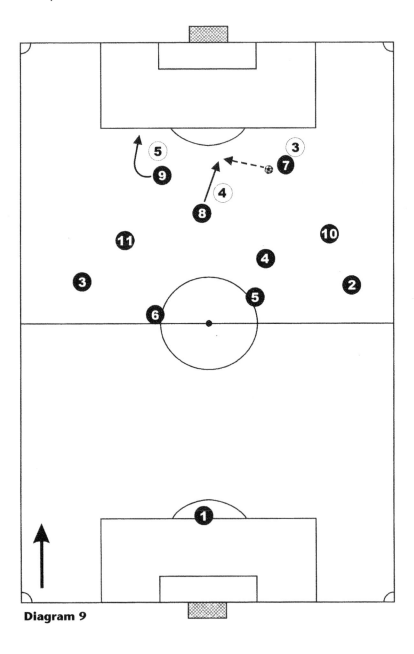

Diagram 9

How to receive the ball

Passing the ball is fundamental to taking the ball towards the opponent's goal.

Effective passing requires good timing between the player passing the ball and the teammate receiving it.

The "receiver" should make himself available for the pass and get towards the point where he wants to receive the ball with good timing, thus carrying out a movement which makes it difficult for the defense to anticipate him.

With regard to the position of the ball in relation to the opposing goal, the receiver can find himself closer to the goal than the ball is. This may happen, for example, when the forward receives the ball from a midfielder.

We say that in this situation the receiver is "over" the ball (see diagram 10).

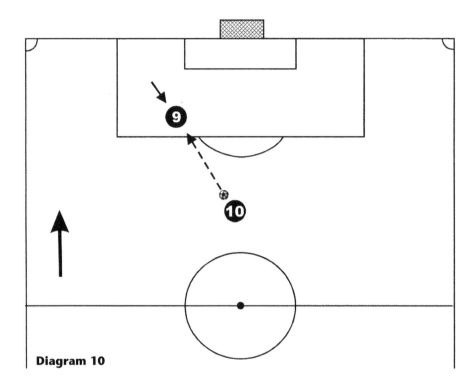

Diagram 10

When the ball is closer to the goal than the receiver is, we say that the receiver is "under" the ball (see diagram 11).

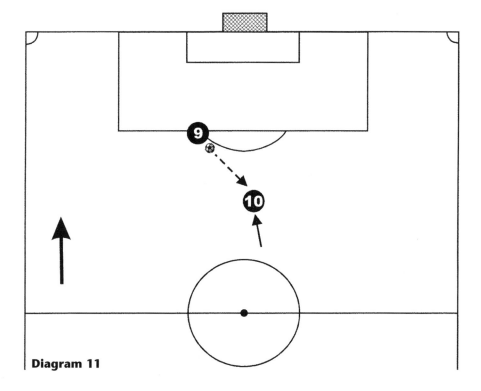

Diagram 11

With regard to the defender, we say the receiver gets the ball "under" when the defender is between the receiver and the defender's goal (see diagram 12).

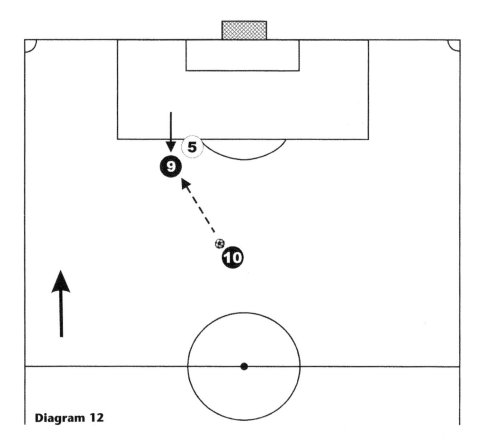

Diagram 12

The player gets the ball "over" the defender when the receiver is between the defender and the defender's goal (see diagram 13).

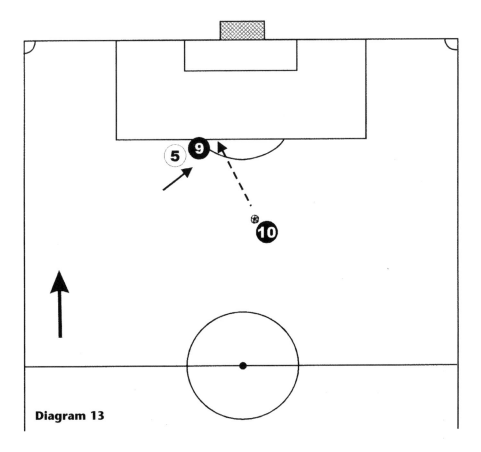

Diagram 13

If the offensive player receives the ball:

"Over" the opponent, and the ball is passed forward, this is referred to as "**depth**".

"Over" the opponent, and the ball is passed backward, this is termed "**penetration**".

"Under" the opponent, and the ball is passed forward, this is termed "**meeting**".

"Under" the opponent, and the ball is passed backward, this is termed "**back pass**".

"Under" the opponent, while passing the ball along the same line, this is termed "**encompassing movement**". (See diagrams 14, 15, 16, 17, 18).

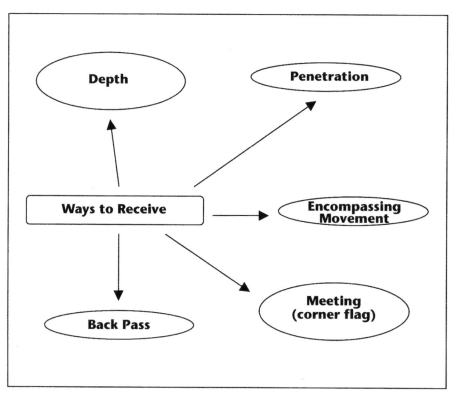

Diagram 13B: The receiving player's options.

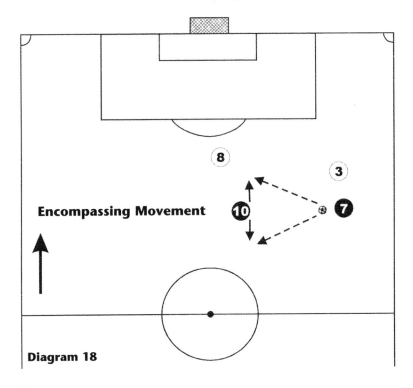

Encompassing Movement

Diagram 18

In the "build-up phase" the meeting and the encompassing movements, as well as the back passes, are very important, while in the "final touch phase", penetrations and movements in depth are fundamental.

Movements of the player without the ball

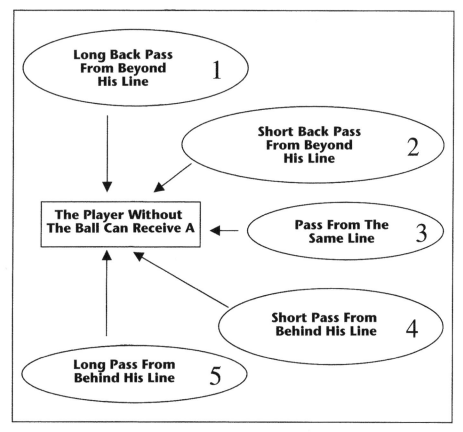

Diagram 19: The possible passes to the player without the ball.

1. If the player receives a long back pass, he should go towards the ball in order not to lose ground.
2. If he receives a short back pass, he should go towards the ball in the offensive phase, while he should take a few steps backward and place himself diagonally with regard to the ball when he makes himself available to keep possession of the ball.
3. If he receives a sideways pass, he should carry out an encompassing movement, that is go forward or backward according to the tactical situation.

4. The front line player (forward) should attack the space between himself and the goal by cutting towards the goal when the teammate with the ball is within passing distance. He should go towards the ball only to carry out a one-two pass or to create space for his teammates' penetration.

5. If he receives a long pass he should nearly always go towards the ball to increase his chances of receiving it and to enable the team to gain ground. He should cut only when there is enough space to receive the ball, as the longer the distance the more difficult for the attacker to make himself available with correct timing.

Two teammates' supporting movements

We will now consider how to organize the movements of two offensive teammates, one belonging to the "attack" section and the other a neighboring "attack" player or belonging to the "midfield" section.

Possible combinations of movements of two forwards

- Both forwards go towards the teammate with the ball.
- Both forwards move forward in depth.
- One forward goes towards the ball while the other attacks in depth.

Diagram 20 shows the situation when both forwards go towards the ball. The player with the ball can either pass it to the near assisting player and make himself available for a combination (one-two) or, as shown in the diagram, pass it to the far forward who can then make a deep pass to the other forward or a back pass.

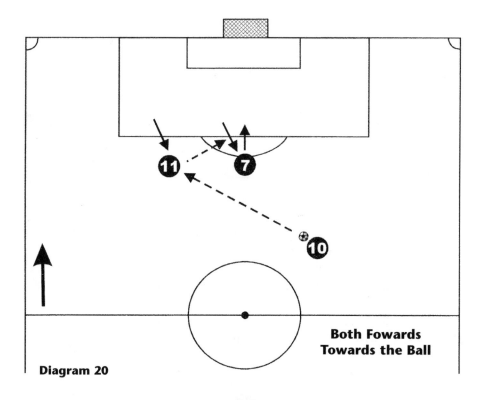

**Both Fowards
Towards the Ball**

Diagram 20

In diagram 21, both attackers go forward in depth. The near attacker carries out a crescent-shaped movement in order to receive the ball. The assisting attacker, who is further away, cuts diagonally into the space vacated by his teammate's movement.

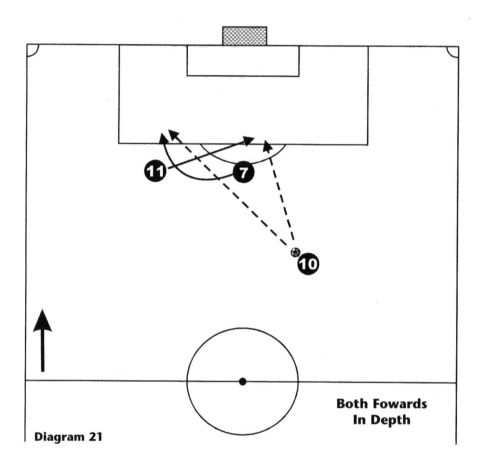

**Both Fowards
In Depth**

Diagram 21

In diagram 21B, the two attackers go forward in depth, without criss-crossing and then cut in the same direction.

In diagram 22 the near forward goes towards the ball, while the far forward attacks in depth. The player with the ball can either make a one-two pass to the near forward coming towards him, or he can make a deep pass to the far forward who is cutting into the space created by the movement of the near forward.

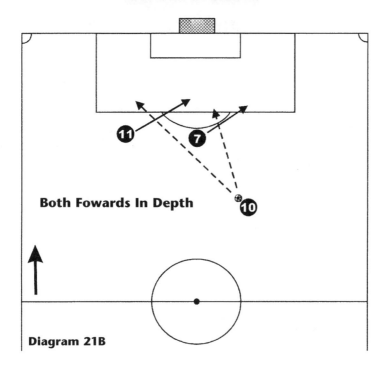

Both Fowards In Depth

Diagram 21B

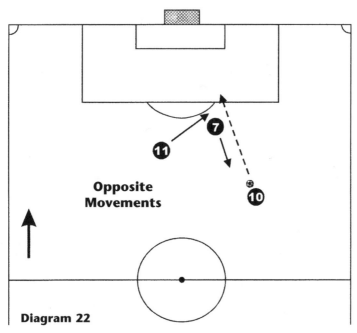

**Opposite
Movements**

Diagram 22

Possible combinations of movements of a forward and a midfielder

- Both players attack in depth.
- The forward goes towards the ball while the midfielder goes forward in depth.

In Diagram 23 both assisting players attack in depth, enabling their teammate with the ball to have two passing options.

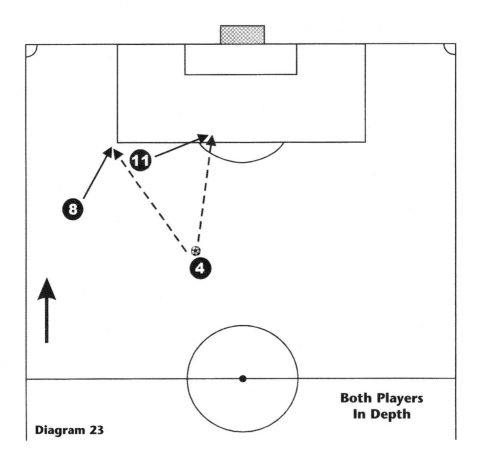

Both Players In Depth

Diagram 23

In diagram 24 the forward comes towards the ball, thus creating space for the midfielder's deep cut-in. The teammate with the ball can either make a pass to the penetrating midfielder or carry out a combination with the forward coming towards him.

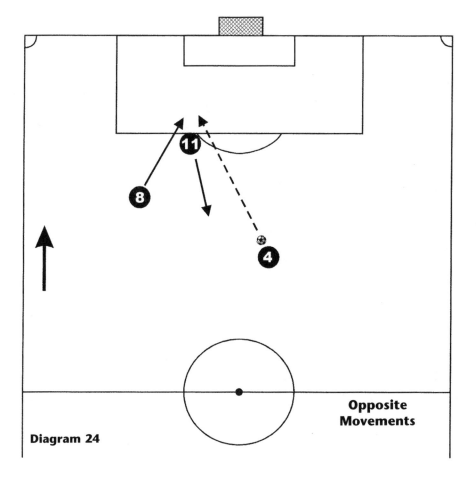

Opposite Movements

Diagram 24

1.2 WHEN THE PLAYER HAS THE BALL

- Analysis of the functions of the player with the ball.
- Passes: specific analysis.
- Dribbling the ball: specific analysis.

A successful team must have players with outstanding skills and vision of play: these characteristics are instrumental to high level performances and positive results.

However, to enable him to be extremely helpful to the whole team, it is important that the skilful player thoroughly understand his functions as well as the tactical importance of his moves.

Options of the player who has the ball

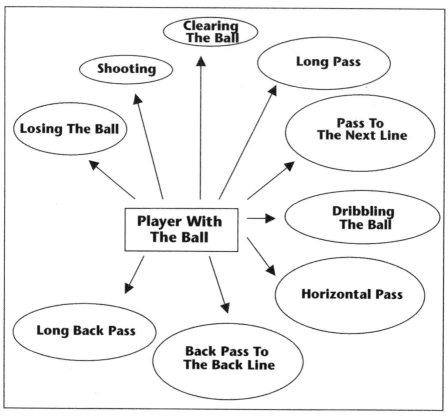

Diagram 25: The possible options for the player with the ball.

The player with the ball has these nine options.

However, if he is in the last line of the offense (back line) there are actually only six "practical" options since the player in this position cannot make a long back pass, is too far from the goal to shoot, and it would be risky to dribble the ball from this position.

Also, the player in the front line (forward line) really has only eight options (since he cannot "clear" the ball), and these are further reduced to six if we rule out the possibility of making long passes and passes to the next line.

A pass to the next line can be made:
1. To a receiver who goes towards the ball or carries out a "waving flag-shaped" movement.
2. To a receiver who attacks the space.

As a general rule, it is better to pass "on" the teammate when he is far away (pass to a distant line) and to make a penetrating pass when the teammate is relatively near (pass to the next line).

Option management.
1. As scoring is the objective of the offense, the player must shoot whenever he can.
2. Considering that the ball must be taken towards the opposing goal in order to score, the player with the ball must do his best to make forward passes, **gaining ground** and **gaining time for the team to stay on offense**. In other words, it is not always advisable to constantly take the ball forward: sometimes it is better to let the offense "recover its breath" by making sideways or back passes, while looking for other opportunities and options, instead of making a forward pass to a teammate in a well-covered area.
3. Another objective of the offense is to avoid actions which risk the loss of the ball. Therefore the player with the ball should dribble while marked only when there is a good chance that this will develop the action, resulting in a shot, an assist or a cross. In other conditions, it is better to make a long pass or to clear the ball rather than to risk the offense losing control of the ball.

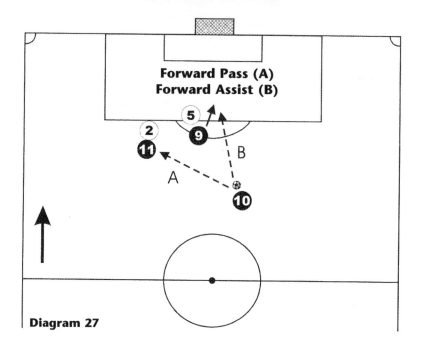

Diagram 27

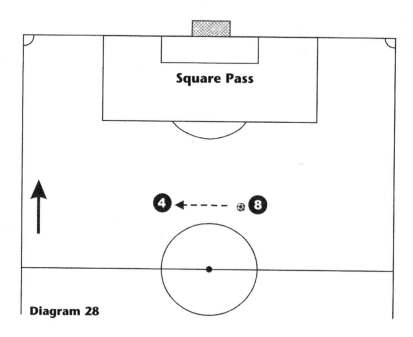

Diagram 28

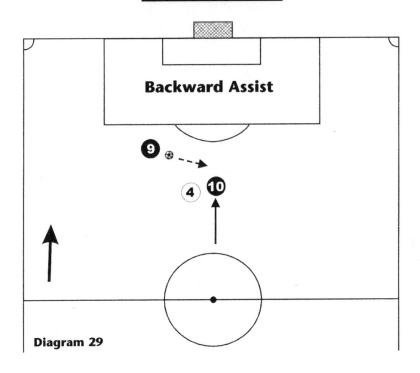

Diagram 29

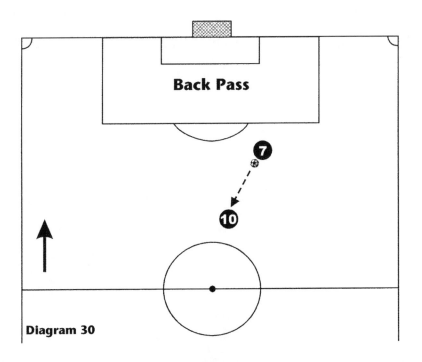

Diagram 30

Dribbling the ball: specific analysis

Instead of passing the ball, the offensive player may opt to keep possession or dribble.

Dribbling past an opponent is one of the most effective moves to create superiority in numbers on offense.

If the attacker manages to dribble past the defensive player marking him, the defense must move another defender towards him. This shortens the distance between the attacker and the goal, and also the time available to the defense to close down on him.

Therefore, dribbling becomes more effective the closer the attacker is to the goal.

The other side of the coin is that as the attacker gets closer to the opposing goal, the available spaces become narrower. This is why the attacker needs to have outstanding skills in order to dribble past the opponent in this part of the field.

It is advisable to try to dribble past an opponent when:

1. The possible loss of the ball does not entail considerable immediate risks.
2. The tactical situation is such that the advantages deriving from successfully dribbling outdo any other option of play (pass, back pass, cross, etc.).
3. There are no teammates available to receive the ball, and dribbling past the opponent seems to be more expedient than keeping possession of the ball.

1.3 OFFENSIVE SUBPHASES

- After gaining possession of the ball.
- Building up play.
- Final touches.
- Shooting.

Today's soccer has a very high pace. The time available to the offensive player with the ball to pass, dribble or shoot is getting shorter and shorter, just as time is getting shorter for the offensive players without the ball to carry out unmarking movements.

In the next pages we are going to consider the tactical steps necessary to score goals, keeping in mind that individual skills are enhanced by well organized team play.

Definition and objectives of the offensive subphases

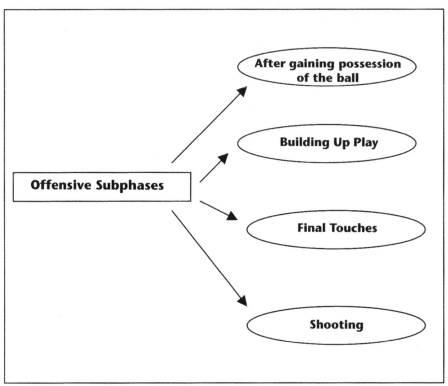

Diagram 31: The subphases of the offensive phase.

After gaining possession of the ball: here, the team has stolen the ball and the player in control of the ball must be in a position to play it, either himself or through a pass to a teammate.

Building up play: here, the team is involved in getting closer to the opposing goal, while trying not to lose possession of the ball (the players should be extremely careful not to lose it in dangerous areas or situations).

Final touches: here, the team is trying to get one player unmarked in order to shoot.

Shooting: here, the team finalizes the action by shooting at the opposing goal.

After gaining possession of the ball

After gaining possession of the ball, it is fundamental to keep possession. This transition phase should be coached with as much care as the offensive schemes.

Ball possession is maintained both through individual skills and through passes to teammates.

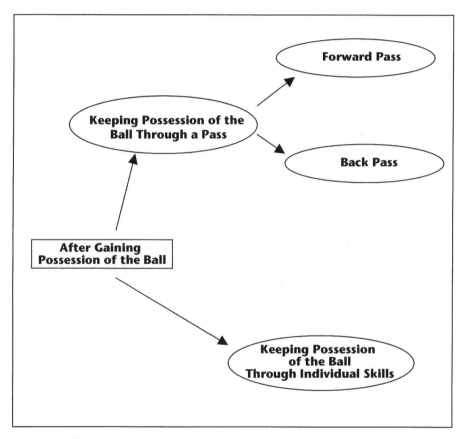

Diagram 32

Building up play

It is possible to get closer to the opposing goal in a number of ways.

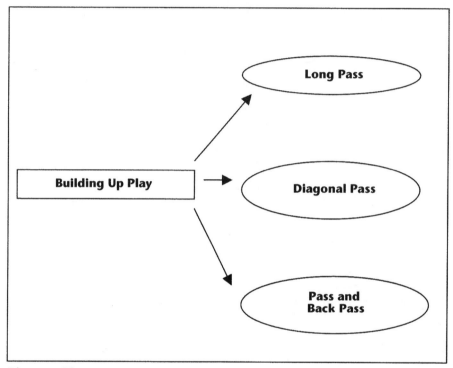

Diagram 33

Let's consider the main ones.

Long pass: this refers to a pass from the zone near the team's penalty area to the forwards, searching for the forward's wall pass or dribble.

A long pass is the least risky way of building up play and it enables the team to quickly counterattack. It requires defenders with good kicking skills, a forward with good heading skills (acting as a target player) and skilful players to get the passes and attack the ball when it bounces.

The importance of the long pass has been recently rediscovered as in today's soccer it is easier to score through quick actions made up of few passes.

It can be effectively applied in the following cases:

- When the opposing team applies pressure and makes it difficult to safely take the ball forward.
- When playing a much better team, the long pass helps maintain the positions without giving space to the opponents.
- Near the end of the game, when the team is ahead and it is better not to take risks.

The downside of the long pass is that the opponents can easily steal the ball.

Diagram 34 shows how to build up play by a long pass to the center forward, who then passes to player 7. Player 7 makes a pass for the quick penetration by side player 10, who tries to take the defense by surprise.

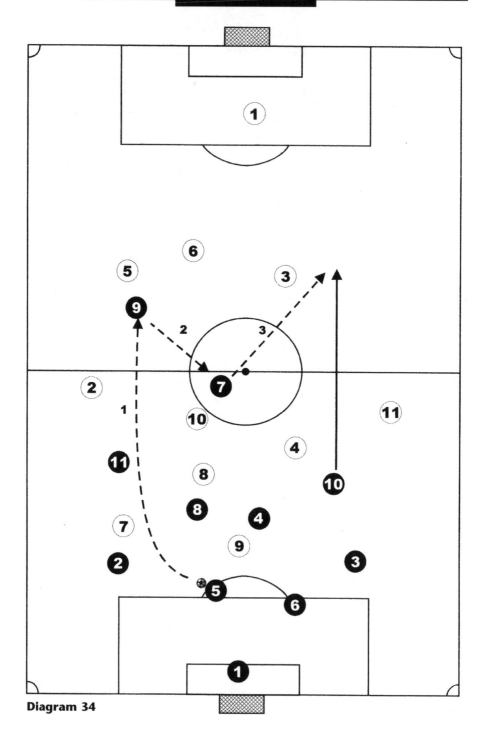

Diagram 34

Diagonal pass: this type of pass enables the team to gain ground and is easy to receive.

It is often used by the backs and the midfielders (the central back who passes to the left or right back or the central midfielder who passes to a side midfielder). By using the diagonal pass, these players can move the ball from a dangerous area (e.g. central zone) to an area where the risks are fewer if the ball is lost (e.g. side zone). Also, the diagonal pass widens the field, thus requiring the opposing defense to move from their positions and "widen" their arrangement.

In diagram 35 the central back (in a team arranged according to the 4-4-2) makes a diagonal pass to side back 2. In addition to adding to the chances of developing an offensive play, such a pass also creates the possibility for the central back to recover if an opponent intercepts his pass.

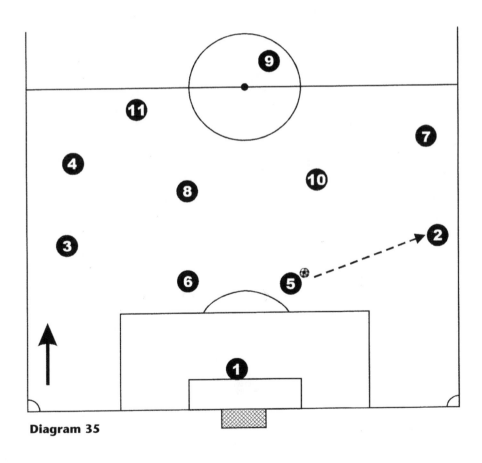

Diagram 35

Pass + back pass: in diagram 36 the player with the ball has the opposing goal in front of him. He can make a diagonal pass to the right or to the left, or a vertical forward pass. He is in an ideal situation since he has the choice of three teammates, in different positions, to whom he can pass, and he can avoid passing along his own line.

In diagram 37 the player with the ball is also in an ideal situation. He can make a back pass to various teammates along different lines - either to the center, or to the right, or to the left.

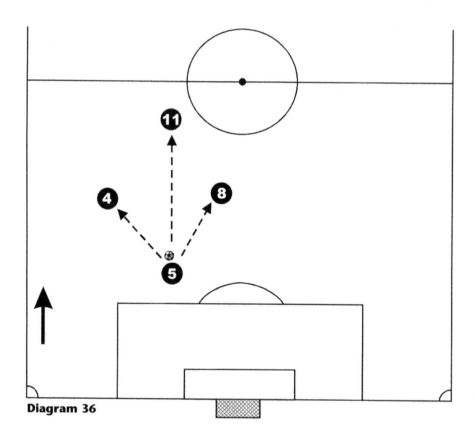

Diagram 36

Diagram 36 and diagram 37 show that the ideal situation for the player with the ball is to be on the top or bottom vertex of a geometric figure in the shape of a rhombus.

Let's see how an offensive action can be built up starting from this situation.

In diagram 36, the player with the ball can send it to one of his two teammates on the sides either by a direct diagonal pass, or by a vertical pass to the teammate on the top vertex who then makes a diagonal back pass to one of them. In the first case only one pass is needed to get the ball to the side player. In the second case two passes are needed, but there is the extra advantage of having more players ready to intervene and defend if the ball is lost on the first pass. Besides, the side player is in a better position to receive the ball and pass it forward.

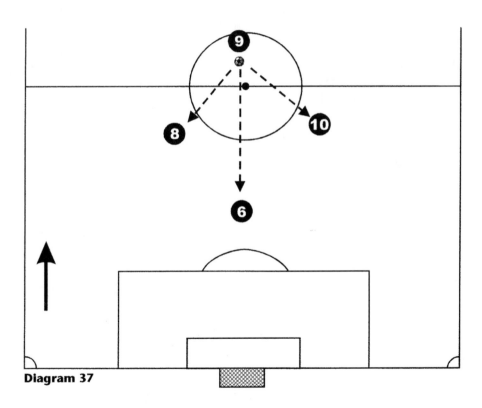

Diagram 37

Let's consider now how the geometric figure of the rhombus can be applied by the teams arranged according to the following patterns: 4-4-2; 3-4-3; 4-3-3; 3-4-1-2.

Example with a 4-4-2 arrangement, diagram 38: the rhombus is comprised of central defender 6, side defender 3, central midfielder 8 and side midfielder 4. Central defender 6 passes the ball to side midfielder 4, who makes a back pass to side defender 3. 3 passes to forward 11 (a new rhombus is formed, made by players 3, 8, 4 and 11). Forward 11 can a back pass either to side midfielder 4 or to central midfielder 8.

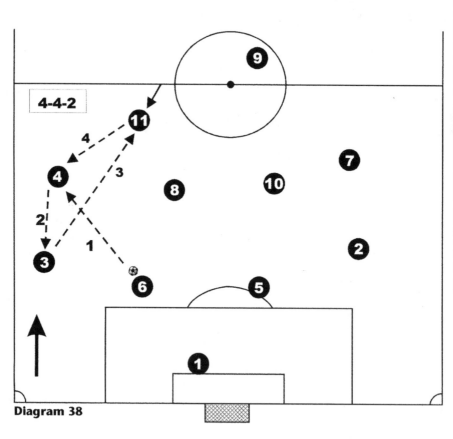

Diagram 38

Example with a 3-4-3 arrangement, diagram 39: the rhombus is comprised of central defender 5, side defender 3, central midfielder 10 and side midfielder 4. Central defender 5 makes a pass to side midfielder 4, who passes back to side defender 3. 3 makes a pass to wing 7 (a new rhombus is formed, made by side defender 3, central midfielder 10, side midfielder 4 and wing 7). 7 can make a back pass either to central midfielder 10 or to side midfielder 4.

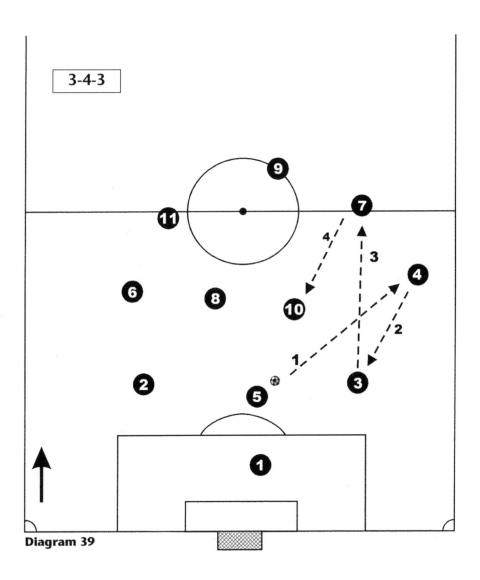

Diagram 39

Example with a 4-3-3 arrangement, diagram 40: the rhombus is comprised of central defender 6, side defender 2, side midfielder 10 and central midfielder 4. Central defender 6 makes a pass to side midfielder 10, who passes back to side defender 2. 2 makes a pass to wing 7 (in this case the rhombus becomes a triangle - as there is no player on the right of the bottom vertex - made by side defender 2, side midfielder 10 and wing 7). 7 can make a back pass to side midfielder 10.

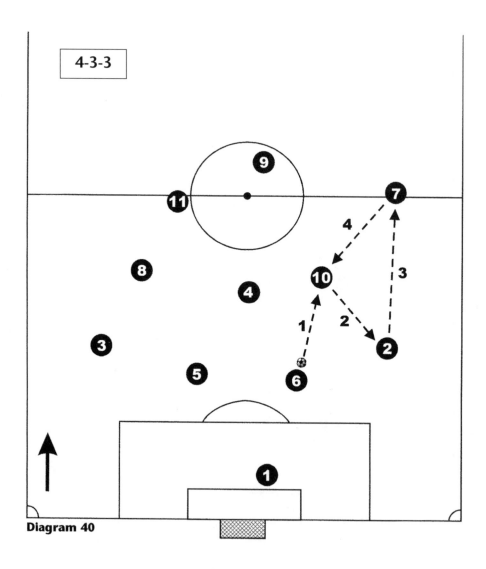

Diagram 40

Example with a 3-4-1-2 arrangement, diagram 41: the rhombus is comprised of central defender 5, center-left midfielder 8, center-right midfielder 4 and attacking midfielder 10. Central defender 5 makes a pass to attacking midfielder 10, who passes back to center-right midfielder 4. 4 makes a pass to forward 7 (a new rhombus is formed, made by center-right midfielder 4, side midfielder 6, attacking midfielder 10, forward 7). 7 can make a back pass either to attacking midfielder 10 or to side midfielder 6.

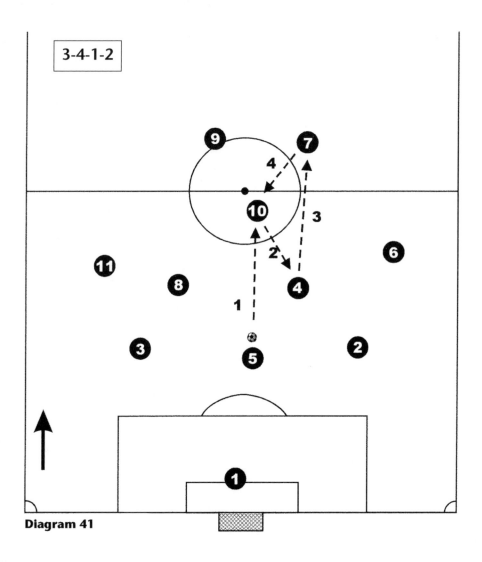

Diagram 41

The general rule to successfully building up play is that the opponent's goal should be approached in a way that avoids losing the ball in risky situations. Some important advice:

- The play should be developed towards the wings through diagonal passes.
- The play should be developed through vertical pass + back pass, exploiting the various rhombuses or triangles that the pattern of play makes available.
- The play should be developed through long passes when the opponent could otherwise steal the ball.
- If the ball is lost, it should be lost only in areas which are not immediately dangerous.

Final touches

The object of the "final touch" phase is to place a player in a position to shoot.

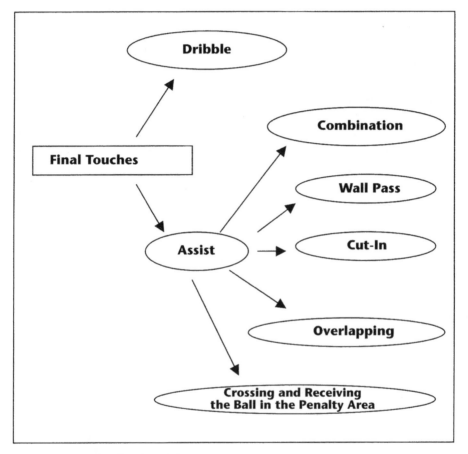

Diagram 42: The final touch.

The offensive player can use the following movements to get free and shoot:
- If he has the ball, dribbling past the defensive player who is marking him.
- If he does not have the ball, freeing himself from marking so that he is in a position to receive the ball from his teammate.

Dribble: a player who is skilled at dribbling and can get past the defender will enable the team to gain superiority in numbers without the help of his teammates' penetration. The teammates can, instead, cover dangerous areas and be ready to intervene if the player controlling the ball loses it.

The player should try to dribble past the defender to shoot or to create superiority in numbers in the offensive zones in order to force the defenders to shift their marking and release their control of his teammates.

Cut-in: here, the forward frees himself from marking and moves to a free space, eluding the defender.

There are several kinds of cut-ins, but three of them are particularly effective: *converging cut-ins, diverging cut-ins, cuts into the "blind side".*
Converging cut-ins are carried out by sprinting towards the goal, with a movement towards the imaginary perpendicular line drawn between the ball and the goal line (see diagram 43).

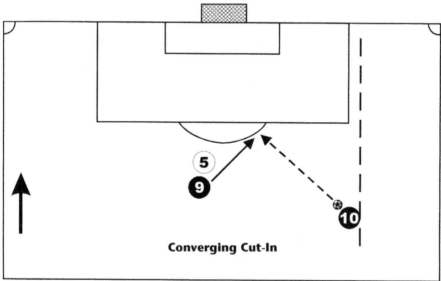

Converging Cut-In

Diagram 43

Diverging cut-ins are carried out by sprinting towards the ball with a movement away from the imaginary perpendicular line drawn between the ball and the goal line (see diagram 44).

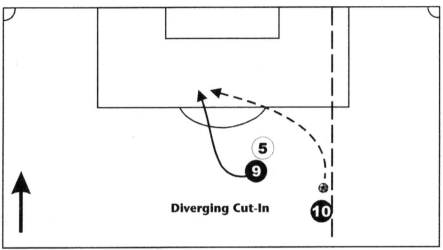

Diagram 44

Cuts into the blind side are carried out by sprinting behind the defender. If this happens, the defender cannot at the same time control both the attacker's position and movement, and the position and movement of the ball (see diagram 45).

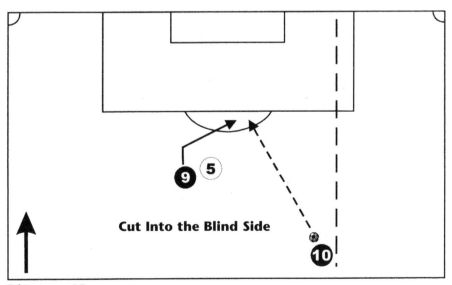

Diagram 45

Wall pass: this is a pass made by a player with the opposing goal at his back to a teammate who penetrates towards that goal. The difference between the wall pass and the cut-in is that in the wall pass the player who makes the pass is closer to the opposing goal than the penetrating player. This is the opposite of what happens in a cut-in.

One of the advantages of the wall pass is that the penetrating player, starting from behind the line of the ball, prevents the defender who is marking him from controlling both the movement of the ball and the movement of the receiver. Another advantage is that the wall pass is easy to receive. One possible disadvantage is that the defender who is marking the player who makes the wall pass can tackle the receiver by shifting the marking.

Diagrams 46 and 47 show the "wall-pass" movement and the possible tackle by the defender who shifts the marking.

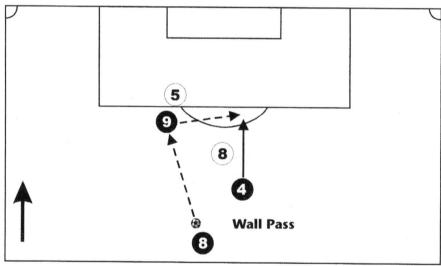

Diagram 46

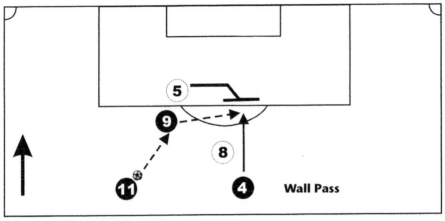

Diagram 47

Combination: this is any kind of movement involving two players. These movements may be "pass and go", "pass and follow", "dummy movement", etc.

This type of final touch is useful against a well-covered or a man to man defense.

Diagrams 48 and 49 show two possible combinations.

In the so-called "pass and go", the player with the ball passes it to a teammate and moves forward, either to the left or to the right of the receiver, ready to receive the return pass. In the so-called "pass and follow" the player with the ball passes it to a teammate, feints to move sideways to receive the return pass, and then changes his run and takes the ball away from the feet of his teammate.

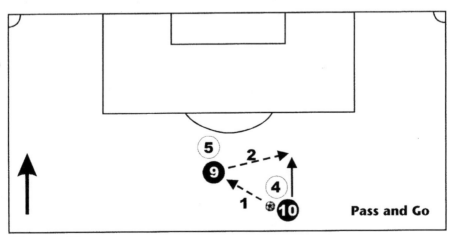

Diagram 48

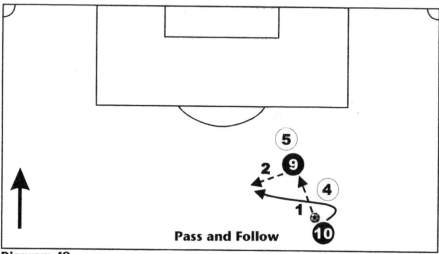

Pass and Follow

Diagram 49

Overlapping: here, an offensive player comes up from behind and then moves upfield alongside his teammate who has the ball. This movement places the defender in a difficult situation, with two players to tackle.

As in the wall pass situation, the player with the ball is closer to the opposing goal than is the penetrating player. The difference between the wall pass and the overlapping is the orientation of the player who makes the pass.

In the wall pass the player passing the ball has the opposing goal at his back (the only other option he has is a back pass). In the overlapping, he faces the opposing goal and therefore has more options: he can pass the ball to the overlapping teammate or he can dribble the ball forward and past the defender.

The overlapping is usually carried out on the wing: in fact, the wing is where it is easiest to receive a pass, while facing the opposing goal, without being tackled (see diagrams 50 and 51).

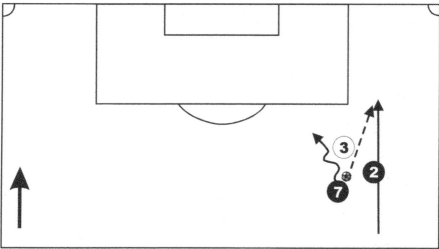

Diagram 50: Dribbling past the defender towards the goal can be the alternative to the assist.

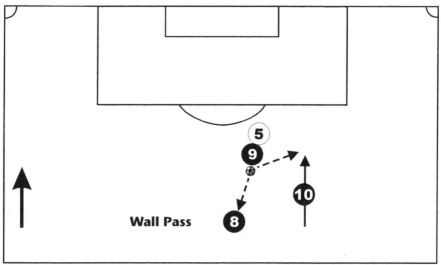

Diagram 51: A back pass can be the alternate to the assist.

Crossing and receiving the ball in the penalty area: the difference between this and the other kinds of final touches is the difference in the kind of marking between the forward and the defender who is marking him.

In cut-ins, wall passes, combinations and overlappings, the penetrating player receives the ball after shaking off the defender who is marking him so that the defender is no longer between the receiver and the goal.

In crosses, it is sometimes irrelevant whether or not the marking defender is between the striker and the goal, since the goal is very close. The most important things are to be first on the ball and to shoot with strength and accuracy. Quite often we see goals scored on a header by forwards who take off together with their own marker.

Even though it is not necessary that the offensive player unmarks himself, he should try.

Diagrams 52, 53, 54 and 55 show some unmarking movements that can be carried out when there is a cross.

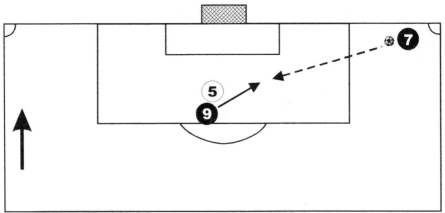

Diagram 52

In diagram 52 the forward attacks the zone of the near post, trying to anticipate the defender.

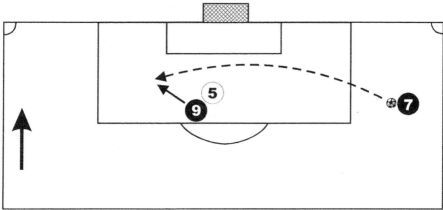

Diagram 53

In diagram 53 the forward breaks away from the defender by moving backward towards the far post. This kind of movement is made easier by the fact that it is carried out on the "blind side" of the defender, who is facing the ball.

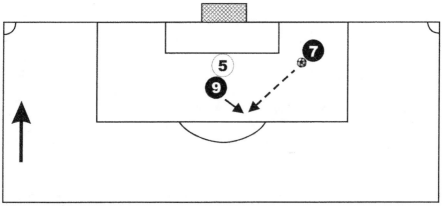

Diagram 54

In diagram 54, player 7 makes a backward cross pass and forward 9 breaks away from his marker by moving back.

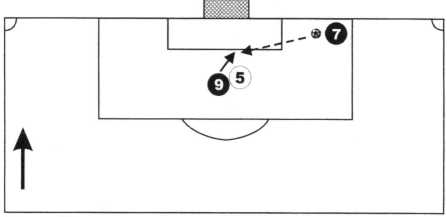

Diagram 55

In diagram 55, player 7 crosses and forward 9, starting from the far post, tries to anticipate his own marker by running behind him.

In order to free himself from the defender who is marking him inside the penalty area, the forward can try to anticipate him in two different ways - from behind or from in front of the defender - or he can break away into the "blind side" of the defender.

Let's consider when and to what zone of the field the player with the ball should pass.

For the defenders it is more difficult to intervene on a crossing pass when the ball is being passed behind them than when the crossing pass is made in front of them. Therefore the crossing pass should be made to the area at the back of the defenders.

For the forwards, it is easier to shoot the ball at goal when it is coming to them as a crossing pass from the goal line than when it is coming to them as a crossing pass from a position futher upfield and away from the goal. In the former situation, they see both the ball and the goal at the same time, and this helps them both to receive the ball and to choose from possible options.

However, it is difficult to make a cross from the goal line and send the ball behind the defenders to the forwards, because the goalkeeper can easily intercept.

Therefore, the general rule is that whenever the player with the ball realizes that he can make a dangerous crossing pass to the back of the defense he should make it no matter his position.

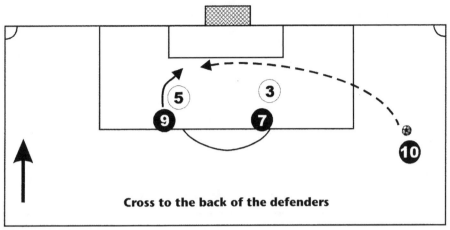

Diagram 56

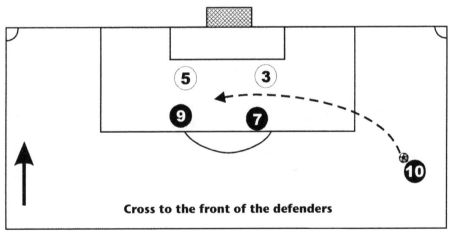

Diagram 56B

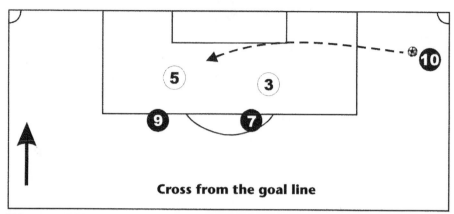

Cross from the goal line

Diagram 56C

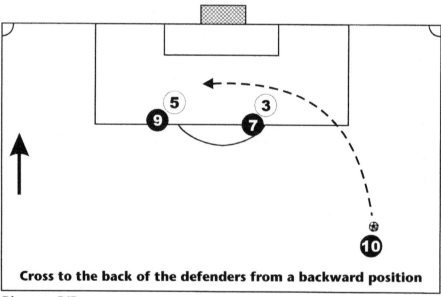

Cross to the back of the defenders from a backward position

Diagram 56D

Shooting

Besides shooting at goal after receiving a pass, it is possible to shoot at goal after stealing the ball or after winning it after a bounce. A shot far from the goal can also be a good opportunity for scoring since it is an unexpected move.

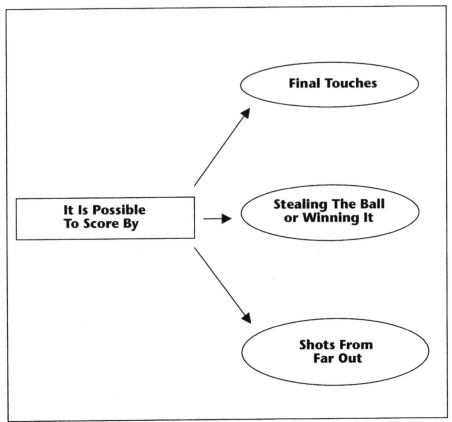

Diagram 57: Analysis of shooting options.

Final touches: a shot on goal can be made after one of the final touches discussed above.

Stealing the ball or winning it: a shot on goal can also be made after stealing the ball or after winning a loose ball. The ball can become loose on a clearance by the goalkeeper, or by a defender, or when the ball bounces after hitting the post.

The coach should make sure that the areas where a loose ball could be won are covered. He does so by arranging the players in an ideal position according to the origin of the shot.

Shots from far out: this is another possible way to score. It requires very good shooting skills.

As for the individual technical and tactical aspects concerning shooting, the shooter must tactically optimize his shot. That is, he must place himself in a position to be able to take the "best possible shot".

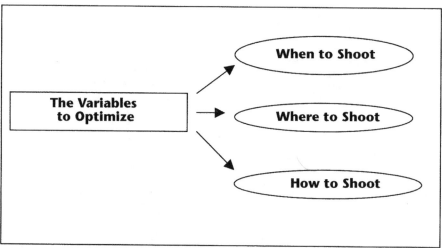

Diagram 57B: The variables that the shooter must optimize.

When to shoot: first of all, the shooter must decide whether to shoot the ball as it comes to him (first time shot) or to stop the ball.

Of course, if he is close to the opposing goal and an opponent is near him, he should shoot on the volley.

Instead, if he intends to shoot only after dribbling the ball, or after controlling it or after dribbling past an opponent, he should choose the right moment.

He should always consider both his distance from the opposing goal and the pressure applied by the defender to decide whether to shoot before the possible tackle by the defender or to shoot after trying to dribble past him.

As shooting at goal is fundamental, the player having a good opportunity for a shot would make a big tactical mistake if he passed up the opportunity to shoot and instead tried to dribble past the opponent.

A similar situation arises when the player with the ball is running towards the goal with the ball and is challenged by the goalkeeper. The choice is between shooting at the point of the goalkeeper's challenge or trying to dribble past him.

If the player decides to shoot at the point of the goalkeeper's challenge, then he should carefully consider the goalkeeper's position. If the goalkeeper is still standing, then it is best to take a low-ground shot. On the other hand, if the goalkeeper is already diving, a lob is the better shot.

Where to shoot: when the player shoots from near the goal, it is enough to shoot the ball anywhere in the goal without searching for the corners. As the distance from the goal increases, it becomes more important to consider both which part of the goal is less well covered by the goalkeeper and at what height it is better to shoot (low, middle-height, high?).

Usually, when the player is far from the goal, it is better to shoot towards the far post.

As for the height of the shot, the player should consider the build of the goalkeeper. An agile and medium height goalkeeper usually finds it more difficult to save high shots, while a tall and long-limbed goalkeeper finds it more difficult to save low-ground shots.

How to shoot: choosing the part of the foot with which to kick the ball may seem easier than it really is. Strength and accuracy of the shot are closely connected to the part of the foot kicking the ball. Therefore, the ability to quickly choose the part of the foot to use to shoot at goal is essential to a successful shot.

A player can shoot by:

- The instep
- The inside of the instep
- The inside of the foot
- The flat of the foot
- The outside of the instep
- The outside of the foot
- The tip of the foot
- The heel
- A header

If the player wants to take a powerful shot, he should kick the ball with the instep, or with the inside or the outside of the instep.

If he wants to take an accurate shot, he should kick the ball with the inside or the flat of the foot.

If he wants to give spin to the ball, he should kick it with the inside or the outside of the foot.

If he needs to take a quick shot from near the goal, he should kick the ball with the tip of the foot. This kind of shot is very helpful in those situations where the player is in danger of being tackled by the defender, or is being challenged by the goalkeeper, since it does not need a "charging" phase of the kicking leg.

CHAPTER TWO
THE DEFENSIVE PHASE

The objective of the defensive phase is **to win the ball**.

A team's defensive and offensive phase are closely connected.
The better a team's defense is at winning the ball, the more opportunities the team will have for a quick and decisive counterattack by the offense.
Just as on offense, it is also important that the defense has a team strategy, so that the players move in a coordinated way.
The necessary steps to winning control of the ball are:
- Forcing the opponents' action towards certain zones of the field.
- Winning the ball upon the opponents' pass.
- Stealing the ball from the opponent.
- Winning the ball subsequently.

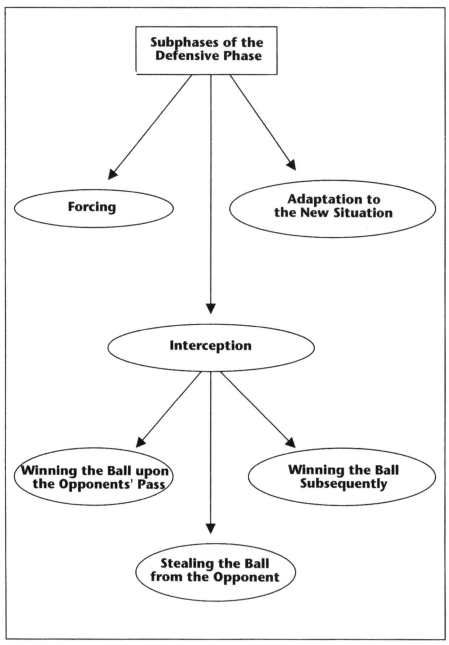

Diagram 58: The defensive subphases.

Definition and objectives of the defensive subphases

Forcing: this refers to a movement which, by attacking the ball, aims at forcing the opponent either to play in a certain zone of the field, or to pass it at a certain time, that is, when the team is ready to intercept the ball.

An example of a forcing movement is when the forward attacks the opposing back, who has the ball on the inside, so as to force the back to play the ball on the wings, where it is easier to double-team him (with subsequent creation of a "weak side" on the other side). Other examples of forcing movements are when the defender plays for time while waiting for a teammate to double-team the opponent with the ball, and when the only space the defender leaves the opposing forward to shoot is an unfavorable position.

Interception: after forcing the opponents' action, the team and the individual player must be ready to steal the ball by intercepting it either after a mistake by one of the opponents or in one of the following ways:

intercepting the ball while it is being passed. After forcing the opponents into a certain zone of the field, the team places one or more players in the position called "watcher". The objective of the "watcher" is to intercept the pass independent of the movement of the offensive player, just like a goalkeeper does when a crossing pass is made.

Stealing the ball from the opponent - immediately: this refers to stealing the ball from the opponent by anticipating him or by a tackle.

Stealing the ball from the opponent - subsequently: this refers to when the defense wins control of a loose ball after a partially successful attempt to intercept the ball.

Adaptation: after the defense intercepts the opponents' action, there is the adaptation phase, with a counterattack if the control of the ball is won, or a return to one of the previous phases if the control of the ball has not been won yet.

Role of the player involved in the defensive phase

When the team is on defense, one or two players are involved in tackling the opponent with the ball, while the rest of the team is involved in intercepting the opponent's possible pass.

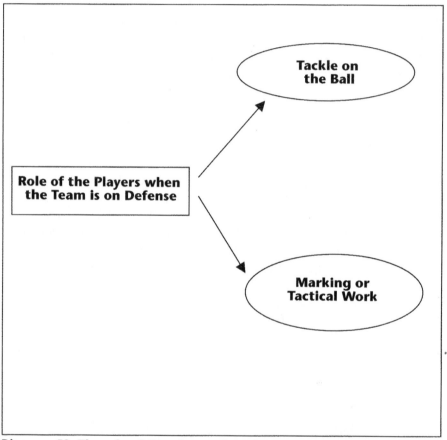

Diagram 59: The role of the player when the team is on defense.

2.1 THE PLAYER FACING AN OPPONENT WHO HAS THE BALL

- How to tackle the opponent.
- Possible options when tackling the opponent who has the ball.
- When to give space.

How to tackle the opponent

The player (or the players, in case of double-teaming) involved in tackling the opponent with the ball has a very demanding technical and tactical task. He must optimize the technique and the time of the tackle without commiting a foul, while applying great pressure on the opponent and closing off the space in order to make the opponent's development of the play more difficult.

In order to apply pressure as soon as possible on the opponent receiving the ball, the defender should quickly get closer to him while the ball is still on its way.

Once the defender is close to the offensive player who is in control of the ball, he should slow down his run in order not to be outpaced, making his last steps shorter, so that he can correctly position himself. The defender should place himself between the opponent dribbling the ball towards the goal and the goal itself, keeping a diagonal position. This enables him to force the opponent towards the zone that the defender considers less risky.

The defender should not worry too much about the movements made by the opponent with his body (feints). He should try to control the movement of the ball. His main objective is to win control of the ball. In most cases, it is advisable to force the opponent's action towards the wings.

Once the opponent's action has been slowed down, the defender should try to take the initiative in order to complete the defensive intervention by directly stealing the ball or by interrupting the opponents' offensive action.

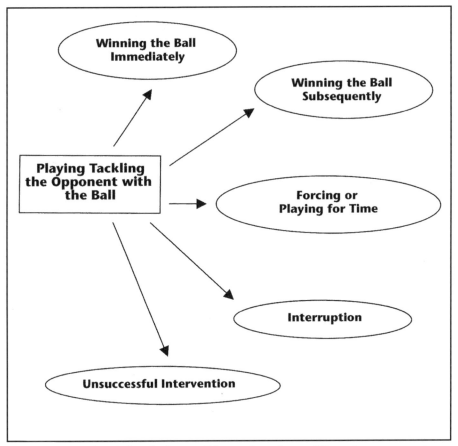

Diagram 60: The defender's possible options in tackling the opponent with the ball.

Possible options when tackling the opponent who has the ball

The objective of the player tackling the opponent who has the ball is to win control of it by a successful intervention.

He may *win the ball directly*: this occurs when his intervention immediately enables him to win the ball.

He may *win the ball indirectly*: this occurs when the defender's intervention enables one of his teammates to win the ball.

The defender's action can also force the opponents' play. This too can be instrumental in winning the ball. In many circumstances, the ability to force the opponent to certain tactical choices favoring the defenders is an important step towards winning the ball.

Another objective of the defender can be the temporary interruption of the opponents' action. This happens when the defender commits a foul or deflects the ball out of bounds, or clears it. This delay of the offensive action may be tactically helpful to the defense, despite the fact that the offense retains control of the ball.

If the defender is *beaten* by the opponent, it is difficult for the defense to adapt to the new situation, so the defender must do his best not to be beaten. Just like it is fundamental to win the ball, it is extremely important not to be beaten.

When to give space

Let's consider the typical situations in which it can be better to give space instead of tackling. In situations of inferiority in numbers it is important to be able to "float" between the two opponents so as to slow them down as they move towards the goal, relying on the team-mates' recovery of their positions. The defender must be ready to take advantage of any possible mistake made by the opponents while the offense is passing the ball, dribbling or controlling it. An example would be a slow or wide pass.

Another situation in which it is better for a defender to give space in order to slow down the opponents' action is when he faces an opponent who has very good dribbling skills. By giving space, the defender can play for time while waiting for a teammate to double-team the opponent.

2.2 THE DEFENSIVE PLAYER NOT FACING THE OPPONENT WITH THE BALL

- The passive player.
- The player active in marking.
- The player active in stealing the ball.
- The player active in tactical work.

Just as on offense, it is very important for the defense to be able to move without the ball. It is the organized movement of all the players involved on defense that enables the team to gain possession of the ball and start a decisive counterattack. On defense, the player not tackling the player with the ball can be termed either "active" or "passive". He is "active" when he participates in the attempt to gain possession of the ball, he is "passive" when he does not.

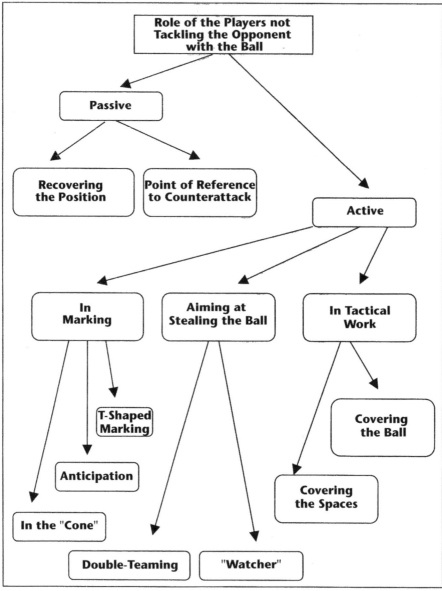

Diagram 61: The possible tactical tasks of the defender not tackling the opponent with the ball.

THE PASSIVE PLAYER

The player who is not participating in gaining possession of the ball is referred to here as the *"passive player"*.

As a general rule, on defense we can term "active" any player who is in the area between the line of the ball and his own goal ("under the line of the ball"), while we can term "passive" any player beyond the line of the ball ("over the line of the ball"). In diagram 62, all the players under the dotted line are "active", while all those over the dotted line are "passive".

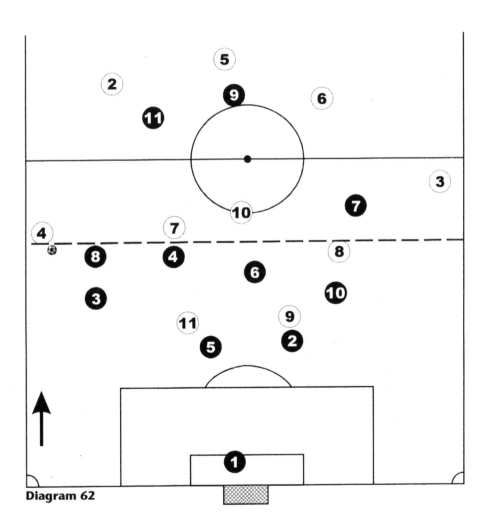

Diagram 62

However, there are some exceptions. The player over the dotted line can also be active when he closes down on the possible back pass, as shown in diagram 63.

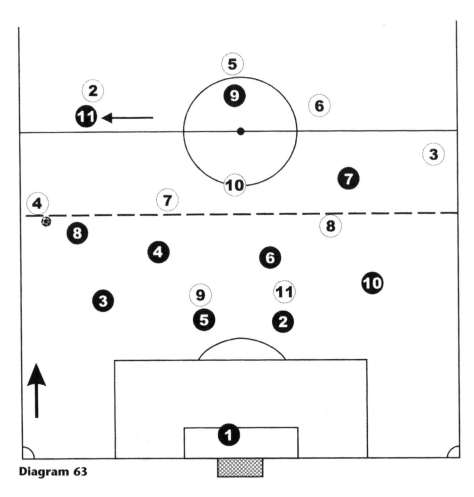

Diagram 63

When the development of the play places the player in a passive position, he should quickly recover to a more useful position which will help his team gain possession of the ball.

Diagram 63B shows the movement of player 7: starting from a passive position (over the line of the ball) he recovers to a position more useful to his team.

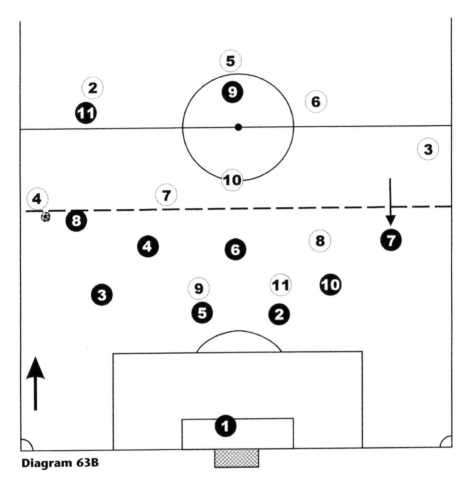

Diagram 63B

The "points of reference to counterattack" are those players who remain over the line of the ball in the defensive phase, ready to receive a pass and start a counterattack if their team gains possession of the ball. According to both the pattern of play and the tactical situation, the coach should specify tasks and strategies for each position, establishing how many and which players the team can afford to keep "over the line of the ball" acting as points of reference to lead the counterattack. Diagram 63B shows players 9 and 11 acting as points of reference to lead the counterattack.

The principle of using the line of the ball to distinguish active players from passive ones does not apply when the offensive opponent with the ball is close to the defense's goal line.

The active player

The active player may be involved in marking, stealing the ball or in tactical work.

With regard to his direct opponent, the **marker** can position himself in anticipation, in the "cone", or in a T-shaped position.

The marker is said to be in *anticipation* when he is between the offensive player with the ball and the offensive player he is marking (see diagram 64).

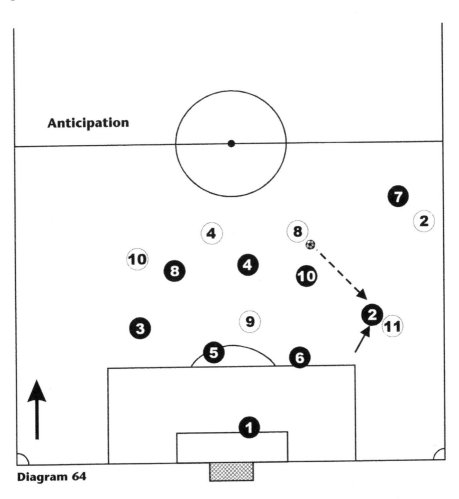

Diagram 64

The marker is said to be in the "*cone*" when he is inside the triangle whose base is the goal line and whose top is the offensive player he is marking.

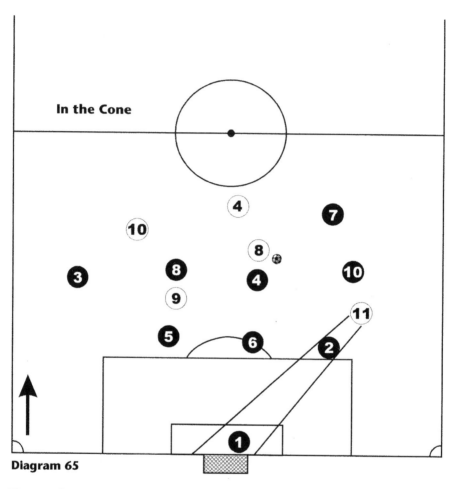

In the Cone

Diagram 65

The marker is in a "T-shaped" position when, on the side opposite to where the ball is (weak side), he shifts towards the inner side of the field.

In fact, if we draw a line between the defender and the forward, and from this line we draw another line perpendicular to it, the resulting drawing is a cross that indicates (with the dotted line) the theoretical shifting line (see diagram 66).

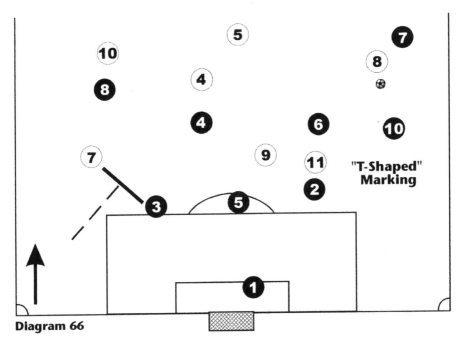

"T-Shaped"
Marking

Diagram 66

The defender usually marks the opponent who is near the ball "in the cone", but sometimes the defensive strategy requires him to place himself in anticipation with regard to the opponent before the ball is passed to that opponent.

In the latter event, the defender places himself in anticipation during the period of time between the moment the ball is kicked and when it gets to the receiver's zone.

The greater the distance between the offensive player who passes the ball and the one expecting to receive it, the easier it is for the defender to anticipate the ball.

The T-shaped marking is carried out by the defender who controls the offensive player on the "weak side" of the field. The T-shaped marking enables the defender to close down on the opponent if the opponent receives the ball in a dangerous area, and to close down on the inner side of the field, helping the defense to be more compact, giving the offense less space to move, whether with or without the ball.

However, the defender should not close down too much on the inner side of the field, so that he can intervene if the opponent receives the ball in a dangerous area for the defense. In diagram 66 the defender is positioned correctly, while in diagram 66b he has closed down too much on the inner side of the field. In that case the opponent is able to receive the ball in the penalty area, since the theoretical "closing line" of the "T" is inside it.

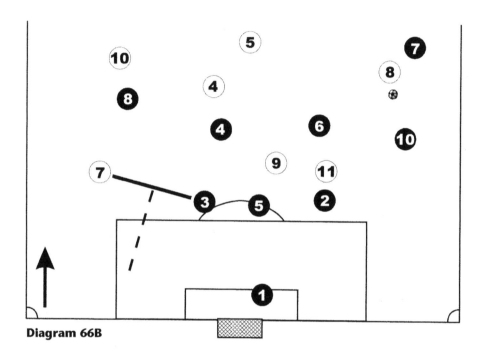

Diagram 66B

The player aiming at stealing the ball

The player attempting to steal the ball can act either as a *double-team-er* or as a *watcher*.

The double-teamer is the teammate who helps the marker, thus creating superiority in numbers on the ball. Together with the marker, he tries to steal the ball from the opponent in possession (see diagram 67).

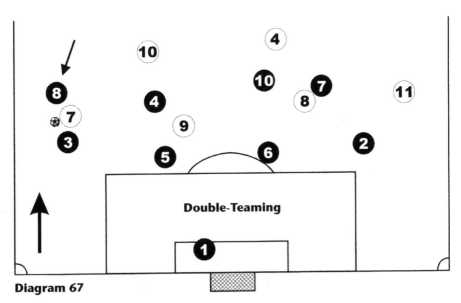

Diagram 67

The *watcher* is the player who tries to intercept the pass. He is near the ball and places himself in a position between the ball and the direction where he expects the play to develop.

The *watcher* does not mark an opponent: his objective is to intercept the pass (see diagram 68).

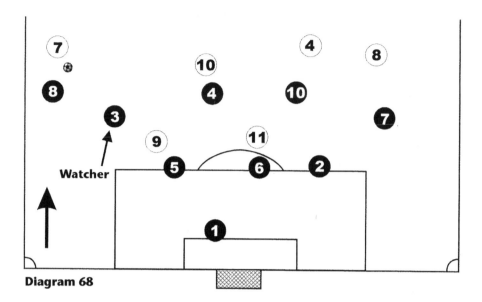

Watcher

Diagram 68

The player doing tactical work

The player doing tactical work can either be involved in covering or in closing off the spaces.

Covering (also called diagonal defense) means going after the ball if the offensive player dribbles the ball past the marker.

A player involved in closing off the spaces does not have an opponent to tackle. However, he remains behind the line of the ball (i.e., between the ball and his own goal) to make it difficult for the offensive players to unmark themselves.

Diagram 69 shows how, in a 4-player defense, the right central back covers the right side back who is going after the ball.

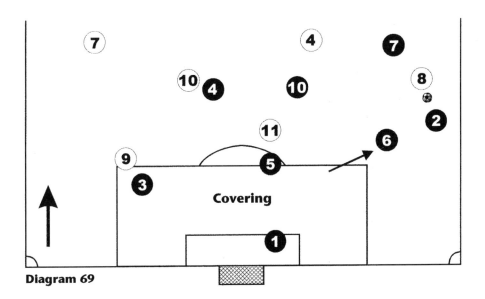

Covering

Diagram 69

In diagram 70 the two side backs get close to the central backs, thus closing off the space to the offensive players who are attempting to unmark themselves.

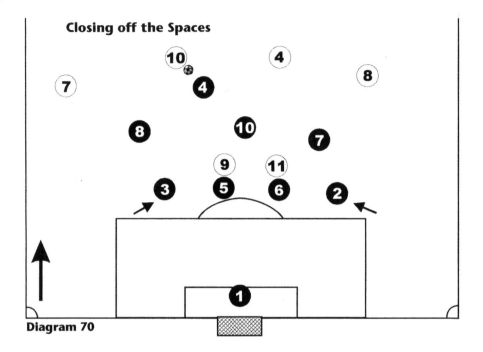

Closing off the Spaces

Diagram 70

2.3 ORGANIZING THE DEFENSIVE PHASE

- Organizing the defensive phase.
- Off-side tactics.
- Countering the offense's final touches.

Given the remarkable increase in the speed of performance in today's soccer, it is vital to organize tasks, roles and movements of the players involved on defense.

How to organize the defensive phase

The main objective when the team is on defense is to win the ball. The ball can be won by:
• Stealing it from the offense.
• Intercepting a pass.
• A foul committed by the offense (off-side, touching the ball with the hand, kicking the ball out of bounds.

To improve the likelihood of *stealing the ball*, the defense should carefully organize double-teaming. The offensive player with the ball should be tackled both by the nearby defender and, if the tackle fails, by another defender (usually from another section of the team).
To improve the likelihood of *intercepting a pass*, it is important to pay attention to the position of the "watcher" (as seen in the previous pages).
The defense must be organized in such a way as to enable the defender to be in an anticipating position even before the pass is made. However, he should be backed up by a teammate in case he fails.

Diagram 71 shows the left side midfielder who double-teams with the left side back in order to steal the ball away from the opponent.

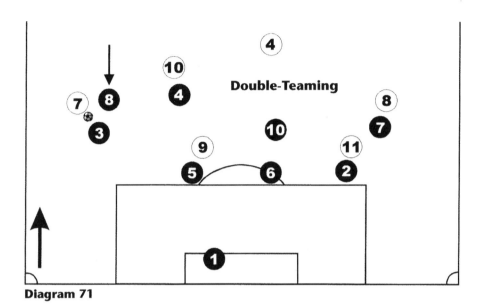

Diagram 71

Diagram 72 shows the left side back who acts as a "watcher" and anticipates his nearby opponent, while the ball is "one-pass away".

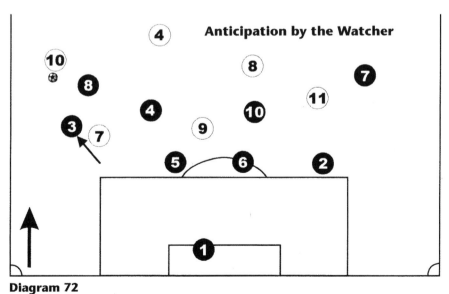

Diagram 72

Diagram 73 shows how the marking tasks should "shift" in case the watcher fails to intercept the ball. In this situation, with a 4-4-2 arrangement, the left central back (player 5) "shifts" and moves towards the ball, while the defensive line is restored on the weak side by right side midfielder 7. It is important that left side back 3, who has become "passive" after failing to intercept the ball, recovers to a useful position either by double-teaming or by placing himself in the center of the defense.

Covering the Anticipation

Diagram 73

Now, let's consider the concept of "forcing".

If we manage to "force" the offense to play the ball towards the wings, then the defenders on the weak side of the field can control the offense by a t-shaped marking. In this way the defense can close off the spaces, thereby reducing both the time the offense has to play the ball as well as the size of the area where the ball is being played (see diagram 74).

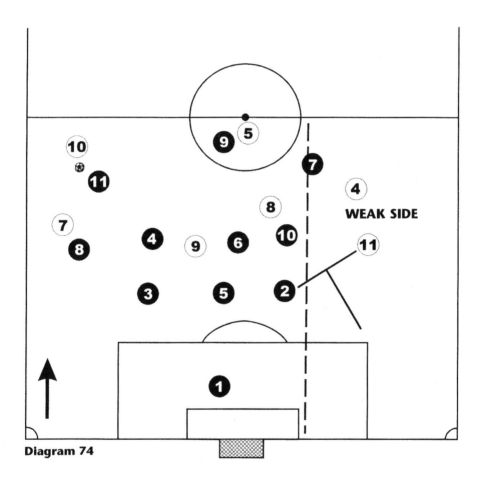

Diagram 74

If we start this "forcing" movement in the offense's penalty area or in the third of the field in front of their own goal, then they will have difficulty in building up play and they might opt for a long pass which could easily be intercepted by the defense.

It is important to emphasize that as the defense line moves upfield, the distance between the defender and the offensive player can be bigger as the defender has more time to recover. This is shown in diagram 75, where a defensive line, made up of only three players, can effectively cover the whole width of the field.

Besides side back 3, covering central player 5 can also close off the space before the offensive player can get to a scoring position (principle of the t-shaped marking).

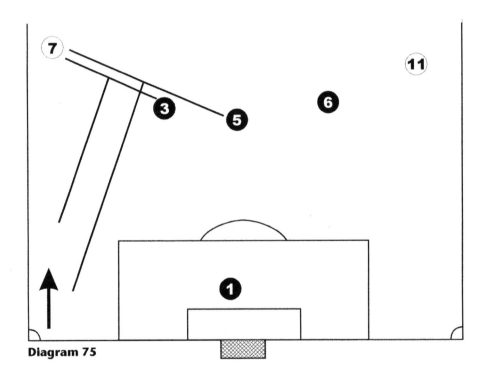

Diagram 75

Off-side tactics

The off-side trap is a defensive strategy to win the ball and also a way to force the opponents' play and keep the team compact in its vertical arrangement.

However, applying this off-side tactic in a systematic way also exposes the defense to the offense's countermeasures, and this can be dangerous.

Coaches usually agree that the off-side tactics should not be applied when the defensive line is superior in numbers to the opposing forwards. In fact, in that event, the elastic movement of the defense should be sacrificed in favor of the systematic application of the off-side trap.

The elastic movement of the defense occurs when it adapts to the tactical situation by moving forward or backward with the objective of preventing a deep penetration by the offense.

By moving forward, the defense can prevent the offense's deep penetration because this increases the probability of the offense being offsides. By moving backward, the defense can prevent the offense's penetration since the offensive players cannot unmark themselves behind the defensive line.

Countering the offense's final touches

In order to counter the offense's final touches, such as wall passes, overlappings, or combinations, it is fundamental that the defense be able to shift the marking.

In diagram 76, back 5 shifts the marking and tackles the forward penetrating after a wall pass.

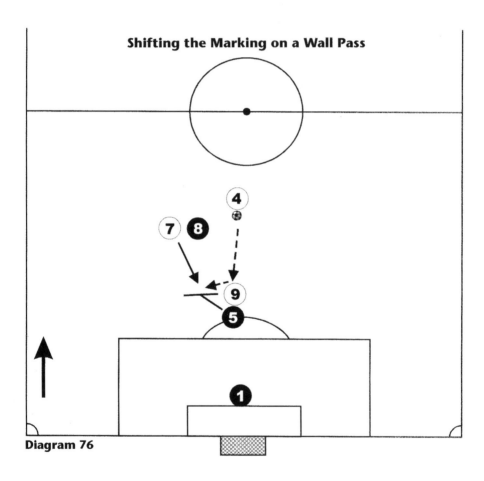

Shifting the Marking on a Wall Pass

Diagram 76

In diagram 77, back 2 follows the movement of the overlapping player, while central back 6 marks the player with the ball.

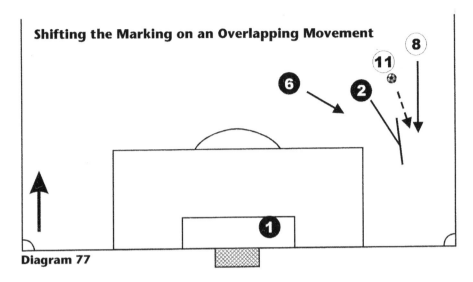

Shifting the Marking on an Overlapping Movement

Diagram 77

In diagram 78, back 5 - marking opponent 9 at the beginning – shifts the marking towards the penetrating opponent 10, while back 4 shifts towards opponent 9.

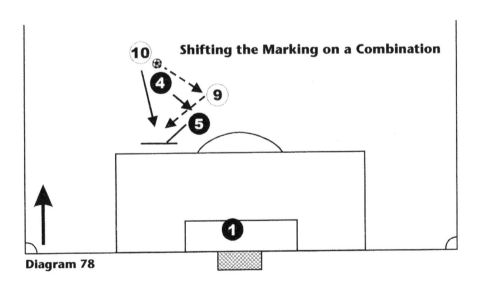

Shifting the Marking on a Combination

Diagram 78

When an opponent tries to carry out a cut-in, the best option for a defense arranged along the same line is to advance, so that the opponent ends up in an off-sides position. If the defense has a sweeper, he will need to cover the opponents' possible long pass.

When the opponents try to create superiority in numbers by dribbling the ball past the defenders, the best options are double-teaming and additional covering by a third player.

Finally, when the opponents make a crossing pass, besides careful marking it is fundamental for the defense to try to create superiority in numbers in the area where the ball is expected to arrive.

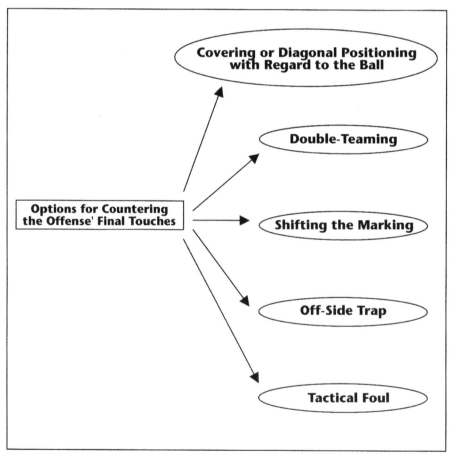

Diagram 78B: The options for countering the offense' final touches.

On defense, it is important to prevent the opponents from shooting. The opposing team can threaten when it creates superiority in numbers. In that case, the options for the defending team are those explained before. Among them, we can also include the so-called "tactical foul". This is the foul that enables a team to interrupt the opponents' action when the opponents are in a very advantageous situation. For instance, when the defense is inferior in numbers to the opponents, a "tactical" foul can interrupt the offense and give the defensive players who are beyond the ball the time to recover to an active position.

However, the tactical foul should not be committed too close to the goal. Statistics show that one goal out of three is scored after kicking the ball in dead ball situations.

CONCLUSION

In every field of human activity, it is important to set goals and to have an idea how to reach them by the means we have available. Such an idea is often the fruit of individual experience, knowledge, personality and insight.

Any idea is the expression of the individual's thought, and is therefore worth respect and attention. However, it is also open to challenge by others.

Evolution and development come from knowledge, culture and discussion. Working out new ideas is extremely important to generate discussion and reflection, eventually leading to progress.

This book contains knowledge and experience acquired by watching, studying, discussing with others and coaching on the field.

The concepts we have outlined are not and cannot be considered as absolute truths. Instead, they are ideas to stimulate discussion and investigation of our opinions.

Variety is a positive factor for soccer, as it challenges every coach and team to face other coaches and teams who apply similar or different ideas. This continuous challenge is a fundamental factor in the tactical evolution of soccer.

Unfortunately, the necessity of positive match results, sometimes even through the use of unfair means, prevents the teams from honest confrontation, thus creating an obstacle to tactical evolution and diminishing the quality of the play.

This book should be considered as an attempt to stimulate a positive and constructive mentality which can express itself through a kind of play whose objective is not only victory, but also respect for the entertaining aspect of the game through a strategy based on the attack as the principal way to obtain a positive match result.

I hope this book will be a contribution to enliven an environment much too often worried only about winning, and that it will contribute to build up a future where the technical-tactical aspect of the competition will be paramount.

Massimo Lucchesi

REEDSWAIN BOOKS

#291 Soccer Fitness Training $12.95
by Enrico Arcelli and Ferretto Ferretti

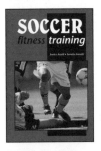

#169 Coaching Advanced Soccer Players $12.95
by Richard Bate

#225 The Sweeper $9.95
by Richard Bate

#256 The Creative Dribbler $14.95
by Peter Schreiner

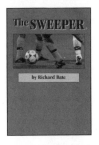

#788 ZONE PLAY $14.95
A Technical and Tactical Handbook
Angelo Pereni and Michele Di Cesare

#793 Coaching the 5-3-2 with a Sweeper $14.95
by Fascetti and Scaia

#794 248 Drills for Attacking Soccer $14.95
by Allessandro Del Freo

#167 Soccer Training Games, Drills and Fitness Practices $14.95
by Malcolm Cook

#177 Principles of Brazilian Soccer
by Jose' Thadeu Goncalves
$16.95

#154 Coaching Soccer
by Bert van Lingen
$14.95

#185 Conditioning for Soccer
by Raymond Verheijen
$19.95

1.800.331.5191 • www.reedswain.com

REEDSWAIN BOOKS

#254 101 Youth Soccer Drills
Ages 7-11
by Malcolm Cook
$14.95

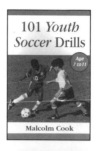

#255 101 Youth Soccer Drills
Ages 12-16
by Malcolm Cook
$14.95

#785 Complete Book of Soccer Restart
Plays
by Mario Bonfanti and Angelo Pereni
$14.95

#261 Match Analysis and Game
Preparation
by Kormelink and Seeverens
$12.95

#262 Psychology of Soccer
by Massimo Cabrini
$12.95

#264 Coaching 6 to 10 Year Olds
by Giuliano Rusca
$14.95

#792 120 Competitive Games
and Exercises for Soccer
by Nicola Pica
$14.95

#905 Soccer Strategies:
Defensive and Attacking Tactics
by Robyn Jones
$12.95

612 Pughtown Road
Spring City PA 19475
1.800.331.5191 • www.reedswain.com